I0453786

Snow

on

the

Desert

Floor

Angela Sanchez

Library of Congress Control Number: 2023923745

ISBN: 979-8-218-33498-7

FOR MY LOVED ONES,
MY BROTHERS,
MY SISTERS,
MY FRIENDS,
AND MY PARENTS.

CONTENTS

THE STARS ALIGNED

Angela Sanchez

Changing of the Seasons.

The bird sings and the bee stings.

The flowers bloom,
and in fall our love did too.

The ice melt,
and love is what I felt. You see me, I see you. And in
spring
you said, I love you.

Yearn.

When you say hello,
a rush of happiness fills my heart. Your voice flutters
in my ears.
And my body begins to crave you, your smile and
your taste.
I yearn for you.

The Man on the Moon.

Our waning love turns in a hue of strawberry red,
our voices intertwine underneath the twinkling lights
of the dark blue skies.

Love reignites. A spark to start, and my heart goes
racing.
It races like horse's, with mouths full of sugar cubes.
I dreamt of a love to become full on a midnight
ocean's shore.

Feelings grow and feelings sprout. What once was
hidden is finally out. I'm not a dandelion;
my roots tether to the ground and you're my magic
hour.
I sought to be picked by you so you can tell stories
of our love
to the future. My garden is for you to cherish, it is
you that waters me.

Your gravity pulls me towards you, my moon.

Tea Leaves.

Tea leaves that I read
and the leaves from the date palm tree. Our initials I
see
at the upper right you're kissing me,
at the edge of the half-moon, at sunset, we are a
team.

My tea cup told me that heartaches and pain will be
tamed.
That our future
is like a daydream.
Love beams, like the heat of the fiery flames of the
rays of the golden sun.

Then, at the bottom of the cup, I see hope,
happiness
and a loving union.

You Like Your Coffee Black.

The freckles on your face I would kiss.
Leave no inch untouched.

Your hazel eyes I would stare. When you called me
honey, your eyes glared.

And your dark hair I loved to pull. Am I dreaming?
You know how to catch a thief, so I'm going to steal
your heart.

Just wait and see.

The Bull by the Ocean.

A king's beach
dark skies and misty nights

grounded by the earth you held on tight

luminous shores and waves' glows

a boat out at sea

and you call out for your queen.

To be Blue.

I can stare out endlessly deep into your blue eyes.
Sight an ocean,
smell the salt in the air.

Hear the waves crashing
and feel the sun
melt onto my brown skin.

I won't abandon ship, my love.
I'm on the bubble,
and I wouldn't mind getting lost in your sea.

Is this how it feels

to be blue?

Noise Complaint.

The sound of the piano echoes in the room. The
song plays loudly throughout the halls of this entire
home.
A noise complaint the neighbors made. You see,
my body is like a piano,
full, rich, and beautiful.
With wonderful wooden brown stains,
And baby,
you're the pianist that plays the keys to my heart so
well.

You know my song. With eyes wide open,
I hear the church bells ring.

I feel your hands all over me,
I feel the strike of G major inside of me.

Make me weak in my knees
with this glorious music. More and more I plead.

Is this how it feels to have faith? What feels so good
can't be seen.

Morning and nights,
even with your work pants still on so tight.

Making music
and it feels so good
when you play the chords and play our tunes.

Petrichor.

I listen to every drop of rainfall
on the leaves of the lemon tree outside my window.
The fall breeze blowing in and I smell the rain,
early mornings sunrises
and I'm in love.

Land.

From red maple trees to palm trees,
I did not know you
from across this vast land. But now that you are here,
holding my soft hand,

I feel the fire, strong.
A fire that burns eternally hot.

Look at the envious sun.
Even mountains move for our love.

Your warm embrace that I've longed for, only in
dreams.
I believed,
and now I'm awake, here in my dream.

Oh, how I feel
with this ecstasy of your love.

When we come together
like the moon at night with the

bright star on the side.

The grass is greener and we are there,

Together.

Wisconsin Leaves.

Wisconsin leaves and the Mississippi stream lovers
throw pebbles into
vivid dreams.

A future
when we dance,
where you fell in love at first sight. Love making all
night.

You confused plastic deer with real ones,
but still hold me tight, my dear.

Desert night
We ride along the road back to our home.

You are lost, and our destiny is gone.

THE DARK SIDE OF THE MOON

Angela Sanchez

.

Push and Pull.

When it rains, it pours.
While I call your name, you shut the doors. When I
speak, you ignore.
It seems like yesterday was boring glore.

Illusions and fake promises.
I don't know what day is tomorrow. Spontaneous
and repetitiveness
while I'm wishing you blow out all my candles.

When I say I love you,

silence.

Apocalypse.

When I was with you,
you knew how to handle the storms of my emotions,
the earthquake of my frustration.
You watched every flower bloom in my garden.

Like the sun, you were fire, and I am earth.
I felt safe, secure, and stable.

You loved the ugly and the beautiful of every inch of
my body and soul.
And without you

is an apocalypse.

Sky.

When the pink sky bleeds,
I breath air of bittersweet.

I dive deep into waters
But I can't touch the floor, sea.

I catch tears with my memories.
I'm latched onto dreams, anchor chains wrapped
and fear pressed against me.

Shooting stars fall
upon my wishes
into the abyss
of loneliness.

A Long Night's Drive.

I may not have you now,
as I weep while driving home. My tears blind me.

I have hope coursing through my veins. Maybe not
in this lifetime,
but maybe in the next.
I know we will be together, with the mess I made.
I promise I will change.

To bear fruit.

The fruit that you want, I don't have.
The apples that are picked,
do you want them that bad?

I don't mind a so-called bruised cherry,
but the fruit you wished I had
I cannot carry.

Bitterness.

I am sure the songs
he sings to you now
are the same ones
he used to dedicate to me.
Can you feel the love tonight?
I can taste my own bitterness.

My Bunny and I.

I fell in love You move along with a woman,
with a different song

You sing a lullaby with me on your side but destiny
died
and you carried on

I weep and I cradle the hope
that lay on my lap

I sing of goodbyes that I can sing along a song
like hers and I

A different life and side
we both live on

It's time to say hello and goodbye

Goodbye, my fellow,
my bunny and I.

Nocturnal.

I'm in paradise, laying by your side,
and if I'm dreaming. I don't ever want to be woken
up

because I'll be without you, and my waking life
will be a nightmare.

You lingered in my mind, and now you reside in a
room that is in my heart.

You crawl into my room at night,
and you haunt me.

You pull the covers and tug on my feet. I see your
shadow eyeing me.

When I'm trying to sleep, let me dive deep
into my slumber

because I can feel the devil pulling me.

Life.

I don't know how to go outside and let the sun kiss
my skin.
How do I tell the wind
to not play with my hair and
whisper in my ear?
How do I let nature know I can't visit her today?

Life makes sense when I'm with you.

Arrhythmia.

My heart is trying to convince me that you're coming
back.
She chants and sings along to love songs
and paints a picture with words of the future. Like if
she waters the blue orchid flowers, they will revive
and have life again.

All the wishing on the shooting stars,
the nightly rituals, and spells on how to bring an old
lover back
that she read from a page at the bookstore.

Praying to God, begging, to return him back into her
life.

She says there's no way that they can't be apart. She
is telling me
that relationships are not perfect,

that he's going to snap out of it,
he's going to leave a cute voicemail, he's coming back
home to tell me he loves me.

But how do I break the news to my heart? That the
flowers are still dead and thrown out.

That she was just another number on his list.
That destiny is gone.
The house is vacated.
The piano is lost.
That the universe stopped listening to her.
God is ignoring her.

He moved on.
He is engaged.
He has a wedding date set.
He is married now.

Might as Well.

You see the world
with blue-colored glasses looking through, empty; no
flowers in glass vases.

You accept no love from the masses. Unpolished
diamond, you show one facet.

I cannot predict your gloomy weather. Cold, and it
feels like rain forever.
I cannot count the stars in the sky nor
see them aligned.
For you, my heart is a design. Yet, dried flowers I
desired.

Wilted.

Our love bloomed
in this dry heat of a desert.
Sand surrounds us.
With a quenching thirst,
we flourish and manage to grow.

We lived in a space where our love strived. Sunlight
beaming into our lives
with moonlit nights. The skies are clear.
We counted the stars and foresaw our future.

As the leaves from our love began to fall, love began
to drink the last drop of our remaining water.

Our oasis was not going to last.
We should have listened to the elements and stood
still past the windy nights.

Hope held on to the last petal, and like a flower, our
love wilted.

Along with life.

Imagine.

There's no way
to take a look into your world or get a glimpse of it.

I will have to
imagine it.

No in-between.

My eyes bleed
they bleed bleed bleed, for what I've seen cannot be
unseen

the sea, I see pretty rocks; on one knee
fluster and flutter
the dreams
to be.

greatly and hollow the beach screech and glass
dive in deep

for the streets won't be clean and the vines tethered

I am possessed

for eyes to turn red and green.

God is Gracious.

Love mocks,
and time doesn't stand still

except the day we shared our first kiss,

the earth paused.

No spells
can make you stay, but the vision I saw won't escape.

Give it another try;
life won't laugh at us.

A Love So Strong,

That it could move mountains, part, and empty the
sea, change the Earth's rotation,
and outlast the sun even after it burns out.

It unlocks heaven.

It can even bring the dead back to life.
Create a new universe.

But in the end, it was just me,
and the walls of this false reality collapse upon me.

Sweet.

You're sweet
and it feels good.

It hits the spot,
but something is off.

Your sweetness doesn't taste like his.

I miss his sugar rush.

Conquered.

This man of many tongues spoke my foreign
language,
a concept that was sought to be discovered.

but he, he knew my consonants, my vowels, and my
alphabet.

Rolled his Rs better than I.
cruel lovers, he writes,
with the stroke of that pen,
maybe he said it in
Russian.

but again, the city wasn't found.

Dust.

Earth and air together,
as the violent winds blew over us,

Nights with endless love.
Promises to keep us tether.

Dust formed in the sky, one moment there
and the next, gone.

The weather has changed,
and so have you.

By sunrise the skies cleared. With the morning sun
she has separated the gloomy clouds and us.

You & I.

The truth is never spoken.
A lesson I was forced to learn.
I, who is now broken.
You, who is pleasured and scored.

Late at night you call my name,
and I forget about my mistakes.

When Pigs Fly.

Serving you coffee in the morning and listening to
the cicadas buzzing in this desert heat.

A glass full of water, I drink.

As you kiss me goodbye, you say that you'll see me in
the late evening.

With a ring on my hand,
you're my favorite kind of weather.

But when pigs fly,
my memories are make-believe.

Thorns.

As we stood together in the garden of roses, I
confessed to you how much I missed you. Longing
to be near you.

As the stars twinkled, My old friend said,
I miss your body.

That moment, I didn't know what hurt more:
thorns that pricked my finger, or your words.

Snow on the Desert Floor.

I know our love is gone
and what remains are the embers of what could have
been.

Hoped
that the mid-Atlantic would be calm as ease
and for our blue skies to turn green. When the last
leaf falls from the old pine tree,

snow on the desert floor

won't make your blood run cold.

THE SUN SEES ME BATHE, LOVE AND SING

Angela Sanchez

Away.

The yellow butterfly flutters away,
a sign for me to sweep my mistakes away.

A Water Sign.

I used to think drowning
was the best feeling in the world

and there was nothing better than my lungs being
filled with water.

Until I realized that I got lost
in this depth of an ocean.

Cold , dark, and blue.

I escaped and gasped for air.

Mirage.

I've crawled into the caves of my thoughts
and I wonder. Lost.
Propelling,
searching for a drop of water.

Aiding for a relief of my dehydration.

Then I come across you: a waterfall, and a

mirage.

An Exotic Bloom.

I scatter through my memories in order to find you.
Time has left us.
Am I feeling blue?

I used to run to you.
I used to look for you
and now I can't picture you.

As the hands of time turn,
I feel true to myself,
and I'm ready for the new.

Call Me Selfish.

Even after the hurricanes of life, the cold from the
isolation,
clouds of sadness
and the thousands of shards from my broken heart.
I won't let it defeat me. I stand tall and proud
because at the end of all of this,
the pain, the dysphoria, and your love.

I put myself first. I found happiness.

I love myself.

Navy Blue.

Pondering into the sea,
a design I treasure so deeply. I long to be adrift
meandering, and you're keen.

I fathom to get lost in this blue tapestry, to dream
endlessly.

With those Pacific eyes, you're my sunrise, you gleam
and I submerge.

Sunken by the storm,
my raft won't make it to shore. Your waves come
crashing in. Horizon lines,
I stood by you and your white lies.
Anchor to an apparition.

Lost, a calling I heard.

I threw myself overboard.
No love boat here, and I swam to the sands. Safe on
the seashore.

The Art of Letting Go.

I get it.
I know, I know, I know,
I'm a screw-up.
I've learned my lesson.
Countless times I begged for you to return.

But you need to stop,
stop taunting me.
You said you're leaving,
so get the fuck out!

When I'm with him, him, or him,
and they begin to kiss my cheek, my neck,
my breast, my nose.
That's when you decide to join the conversation.

You make me feel like it's you.
One moment you're there,
then you disappear.

This needs to end.
Please.
I have to move on.

Love.

I hoped for a love that was so divine that it could
change the Earth's rotation.
I dreamt of a love that was so strong

But,
I've realized I've had it within myself.

Now, I let the moon kiss the back of my neck, let the
wind scream out my name.
Skies turn into lakes, where I fish alone.
I'll stand tall like the mountains that surround me.
Trust me, my world won't stop turning, and I dream
of love worth yearning.

Catching Feelings.

Catching feelings
with the net of my ears and my mouth.

You know what you're doing.

When you speak the first syllable of my name
With the base of your voice,
you draw me in.

I wake up with a stomach full of butterflies fluttering
their wings inside of me.

The tip of your tongue, with that word that you say
so loosely.
It makes me want to stay and say it. But I picked my
poison and I'll drink
until my stomach is flooded
with liquid courage and after it runs its course.
Let's see if those wings will flap again.

2 a.m.

As cliche as it sounds,

I need a stronger drink to drown my sorrows.

Airing Out the Dirty Laundry.

I used to want to feel validated from a man.
And if I was a womanly enough in his eyes, then I'm
good.

Some men had that control over me.

I didn't mind the disrespect,
nor the compliments or the awkward series of
questions if I was good in bed.
That I look good for being a different type of
woman.
If I can give them head, or you can't tell with me
at the beginning of each conversation of meeting
them.

Like I said, I needed that validation. So, I dry-
swallow the pill.
After having the same routine,
I gave up and grew tired of it.
When I give advice to my friends and not take my
own.

I had realized
I needed to be respected

and I don't need a man to tell me something

I already know.
I might sound vain, but I'm proud of myself. Who
pushed me to start my transition?
Me.
Who went to the doctors and sought out a therapist?
Me.
Who goes out at night risking to put her life in
danger because of who I am?
Me.
At the end, I have myself.
I got me.

I motivated myself.

Which one of these men who felt entitled
helped me? None.
As I know better now, I don't need that disrespect.

I don't need a hero,

and I don't need a man to validate my womanhood.

Because he might be a nice guy, but he ghosted me
for months.

Just 'cause you walked me to your front door after
having sex, you're still a dick.

Or my favorite,

you say you don't want anything serious, and there
you are, treating me like a girlfriend, kissing me,
calling me baby, letting you cum inside me,
and you act like you respect me.

I love myself.
I don't need that in my life.

Venus in Leo.

This unrequited love deals with pride as well.

As you can tell I look cool and
act like I don't care.

This pain is in a box inside of me, scratching its way
out.
My facade won't be ruined,
so I won't let my inner lion roar, and I will close one
more door.

Woman.

As the words slipped out of my mouth,
I am a woman,
the pain and the somberness flooded my mind.

How these simple words can change my life.

My mother and her silence
as we sat in my room.
No tears, no anger.
Was this just the eye of the storm? Was she gonna
release her wrath and drown me?
Is she not going to love me?

As the seconds gone by,
my heart was screaming.
Then I felt nothing
but light and peace,
coming from her and from within.
I knew she saw me the way I see myself: a woman.

Femme Fatale.

I build a fantasy
and hope for the best.
My heart takes the shot
bang..

You pick up the pieces
and start to chip the paint away.

The film is done,
but there's a plot twist.

I'm the one who breaks
your heart at the end.

A Play on Words.

Anguished by the pages of the book. Paper cuts I caused.

Detached.

I don't want to read any further.
I'm tired of this story.
I don't want to know anymore. I don't want to hear anymore.

Anymore.

Sounds like a broken record Repeating the same words and the same memories.

A stain on my heart.
Visions stuck in a narrow tunnel. Finding the light and yearning hours.

It's a long stretch to get there.

Curiosity Killed the Cat; the Dog, the Black-Tailed Jackrabbit, and the Desert Tortoise.

To the death,
the tale, it's over. Endings.
Tears on the blue orchid's petals while the owl sets
flight
and desires burn out.

Witch.

You strike your finger that's full of rage.
rumors spread like a forest fire.
I'm the one to be burned at a stake? you caused a
friendly fire.

whisper, whisper that my dress is laid
I could tell
is what you said, a night of outing
till the morning sun rays it's not what you said,
flowers bloom
I'm not made of clothes or perfume.

it's my story to tell my world to show,
you have no saying in this and it's true, the sky is
blue.

greed blinded you
and a green-eyed monster to
you force me out
and accused me of a witch.

well, this bitch
will still fly on her broom.

Goodbye in Silence.

Like ice in my hands, I couldn't hold you any longer.
That was all I could face. In my heart,
I stored your warm embrace.

I examined your face, kissed your neck, and smelled
your clothes.

Because I was letting you go, and I wasn't coming
back.
I was saying
goodbye in silence.

Imagine Pt. 2.

Revisiting old wounds and picking at the scab
won't help the healing process.

Closure is what I need, showing off my new scars, I
believe.

I imagine you in line at the grocery store where we
roamed,
tapping you on your shoulder with a warm hello.
Snow did fall in the desert, yet still no hope.
We catch up in the parking lot with laughter,
and I imagine we'd elope.

What was said from your father,

farewell kisses on the cheek send you off with
happiness because I learned to love
and a goodbye embrace.

Closure that I've imagined because reality is not keen.

Happiness.

I don't miss you,
I just miss the idea of you being there, missed you
being the void.

I am Ms. and won't be your Mrs.

I've learned to fill those holes in my heart with soil
and planted seeds of love.

Now I watch them grow every spring, I watch them
sprout.
I watch the leaves fall
and prepare for the harvest:
in bloom again.

You won't water me again,
nor will my tears water my garden. The only water I
need is from my own happiness.

The Archer.

At the end of the heartbreaks and discovering my
love within,
I'm on the path of happiness and riding on the
archer's back.
Cupid shot his arrow, striking me deeply within.
Gold poured out, and my love did too.

The centaur possessed my heart, and I was in love...

But with the high I felt, mounted, he knocked me
down.

Hamal.

I long for the nights when I lay my head on your
chest
and I hear your heart speak. Love is what he
confesses.
I see the waves of the ocean, and then the sea takes
you away from me.

I wait.

You've returned, my brightest star.
I've held onto the memories we made,
I held on to our future we created,
this wonderful world we built.
I kept our love anchor to my heart.
We can't be apart.
But I feel it again.
The Universe pulls you away from me again.

I wait.

You're back, my old soul lover.
The stars have aligned again.
I held the coins from the places you visit. I held on
to the promise you and I made. Destiny brought us
back again.

Times passes winter to spring.

Time passes, and I sense gravity from
outside is approaching.
You're leaving again? Is this our fate?

To walk two paths separately never on one?
The two sides of a coin, the day and night we are.

The heavens roar,
and I hold on.

But hope is a double-edged sword, and I need to let
you go.

I'm letting you go.

After the Storm.

Peace, love, clarity, patience, and strength.
I pray to God to give me
peace, love, clarity, patience, and strength.
Now, I'm moving forward in life with

my peace, my love, my clarity, my patience,
and my strength.

Summer.

The snow on the mountaintops had melted, and so
did our love.
The bee's sting lingers,
and the singing birds sleep. The miles that were apart
now feel far and far,

so it is best to keep my heart...

Angela Sanchez

ABOUT THE AUTHOR

Angela Sanchez, a poetic soul from the enchanting Coachella Valley, invites readers on an introspective journey through her debut collection,
Snow on the Desert Floor.
Within its pages, Angela's words gracefully dance around the themes of love, heartbreak, and relationships, all while nature serves as a constant backdrop, enhancing the emotions conveyed in her words. Get ready to be captivated by Angela's heartfelt poetry and prose of the human experience.

Angela Sanchez